FAMILY WALKS AROUND FLEET, CROOKHAM AND CRONDALL

CONTEN

ABBREVIATIONS

INTRODUCTION

Walk No 1	CROOKHAM & DOGMERSFIELD		
Walk No 2	BEACON HILL & EWSHOT	4 Miles	6
Walk No 3	BRAMSHOT & MINLEY	4 Miles	8
Walk No 4	ITCHEL MILL SPRINGS	4 Miles	10
Walk No 5	CRONDALL	4 Miles	12
Walk No 6	BARLEY MOW & CROOKHAM	4 Miles	14
Walk No 7	WINCHFIELD & DOGMERSFIELD CHURCHES	4 Miles	18
Walk No 8	ELVETHAM	3½ Miles	20
Walk No 9	BASINGBOURNE & ZEBON	3 Miles	22
Walk No 10	CRONDALL & THE HARROW WAY	4 Miles	24
Walk No 11	HORSEDOWN COMMON & THE MAULTHWAY	4 Miles	26
Walk No 12	CRONDALL & LEE WOOD	4 Miles	28
	Location of Walk Starting Points		16/17
	POINTS OF INTEREST		30

Published by
FOOTMARK PUBLICATIONS
12 The Bourne, Fleet, Hampshire

FAMILY WALKS SERIES

Family Walks around Fleet, Crookham & Crondall   ISBN 0 9527363 7 3
Family Walks around Farnham & the Hampshire Borders 2001
Family Walks around the Blackwater Valley 2000
Family Walks around Hook, Hartley Wintney & Rotherwick 1999
Family Walks around Odiham & Upton Grey 1998

© Footmark Publications. All rights reserved. No part of this publication may be reproduced in any form or by any means (except short passages for review) without the prior written permission of the publisher.

Great care has been taken to be accurate. The publisher cannot however accept any responsibility for errors which may occur, or their consequences. All walk descriptions have been checked independently, but changes can occur. **If any problems are encountered on the walks, please report to the Rights of Way Officer asking for the problem to be cleared. Give a map reference if possible.**

Rob Thompson,
Rights of Way Officer
The Old College,
College Street,
Petersfield,
Hampshire GU31 4AG
Tel: 01730 235824

ABBREVIATIONS
R   Right   RHS   Right hand side
L   Left   LHS   Left hand side

INTRODUCTION

This book covers twelve circular walks in the attractive countryside around Fleet, Crookham & Crondall. Some of the walks were included in earlier Family Walks Series books, but these have been revised to take account of changes that have occurred or the routes somewhat altered. The usual format of the walk description and accompanying map on facing pages is retained. Paragraph numbers correspond to numbers on the maps. Points of Interest seen on the walks are described separately at the end of the book.

Starting points for the walks (where parking should be available) are shown on a map in the centre pages of the book. However all of the walks can be started from any point on the walk and indeed for some walks alternative start points are indicated. Ordnance Survey Explorer Maps Nos 144 & 145 at a scale of $2\frac{1}{2}$ inches to the mile show all the footpaths used in the walks in detail and allow variations in the walks should this be desired. However the maps included in this book give adequate guidance.

Most of the walks pass public houses where refreshments are available. Please ask the landlord for permission if you wish to leave your car in the pub car park (and remember to use the hospitality!)

In dry conditions good walking shoes should suffice, but wellies may be needed in wetter conditions. Dog owners please keep your dog on a lead where livestock is present and it is probably wisest to avoid fields with livestock and their young.

Some walks pass close to private houses - please respect the residents' privacy.

My thanks to Ted Blackman for his sketch maps (based on out of copyright maps and path surveys) and to the following for checking the walks: June & Mark Beckley, Harley Davies, Jane & David Eccles, Carol Coleman & June Beckley, Bridget & Ted Payne, Pat Sansom and Pam & Steve Turner. Finally to my Wife Kathleen for helping me to survey the walks.

Bob Rose
November 2001

Walk No 1   CROOKHAM & DOGMERSFIELD

[4 miles, 2 hours]

1. Start from the Crookham Village WI Hall next to Crookham Street Social Club. Return to The Street and turn L along the road passing The Black Horse. Cross over The Street to the footway opposite and continue ahead. A few yards beyond Veronica Drive look out for a footpath signpost on your R. Turn R along an enclosed path, go through a small metal gate and follow the enclosed path between fields. Go through a chicane, turn R through a gap and along the path on the edge of the wood. At a stile on your R, turn L on the track through the wood and over a sleeper footbridge to reach the road.

2. Turn R along the road, go over Poulters Bridge, bear R and soon cross over the River Hart. Pass Burnt House on your R followed by a footpath signpost. Turn R along the enclosed path to reach Crondall Road. Turn R along the road, go over Chequers Bridge [Walk can be started here from the canalside carpark] and pass the George & Lobster. In 250 yards pass Stroud Lane on your L, and in a further 120 yards cross a bridge with white rails. Shortly opposite Brook House, turn L over a stile by a footpath signpost to Dogmersfield.

3. Go across the field initially with the fence on your L. Continue ahead over a stile [with a waymark] and footbridge to the next field. Head for its RH corner, cross the stile by the iron gate, turn R along a wide track between fences. At the front of the bungalow, turn R along the metalled track to reach the road.

4. Turn L along the road to Dogmersfield [keep ahead for a few yards to visit the Queens Head] and shortly turn R at a footpath signpost. Follow the enclosed path by a stream, over a stile and continue on the enclosed path leading to a gap. Cross the wide track and keep ahead with the River Hart on your L and a fence and then trees on your R. Enter a large field, turn R along the RH field edge. At the oak tree on your R, keep ahead across the field aiming for the LH end of a line of trees. Cross the footbridge and stile to the next field, turn half L diagonally across the field [go round the LH edge of the field if wet] and over a stile and footbridge to reach Hitches Lane.

5. Cross the road carefully, turn L along the footway and in 50 yards turn R over a stile by a gate and footpath signpost. Follow the LH field edge; leave the field by a gap next to a stile, turn R along the track and in 400 yards at the end of a field, turn R along the LH edge of the field. In 100 yards, turn L through a gap along an enclosed path. Turn L along the LH edge of the field, over a stile and turn diagonally half R across the next field. Cross the stile to return to the start.

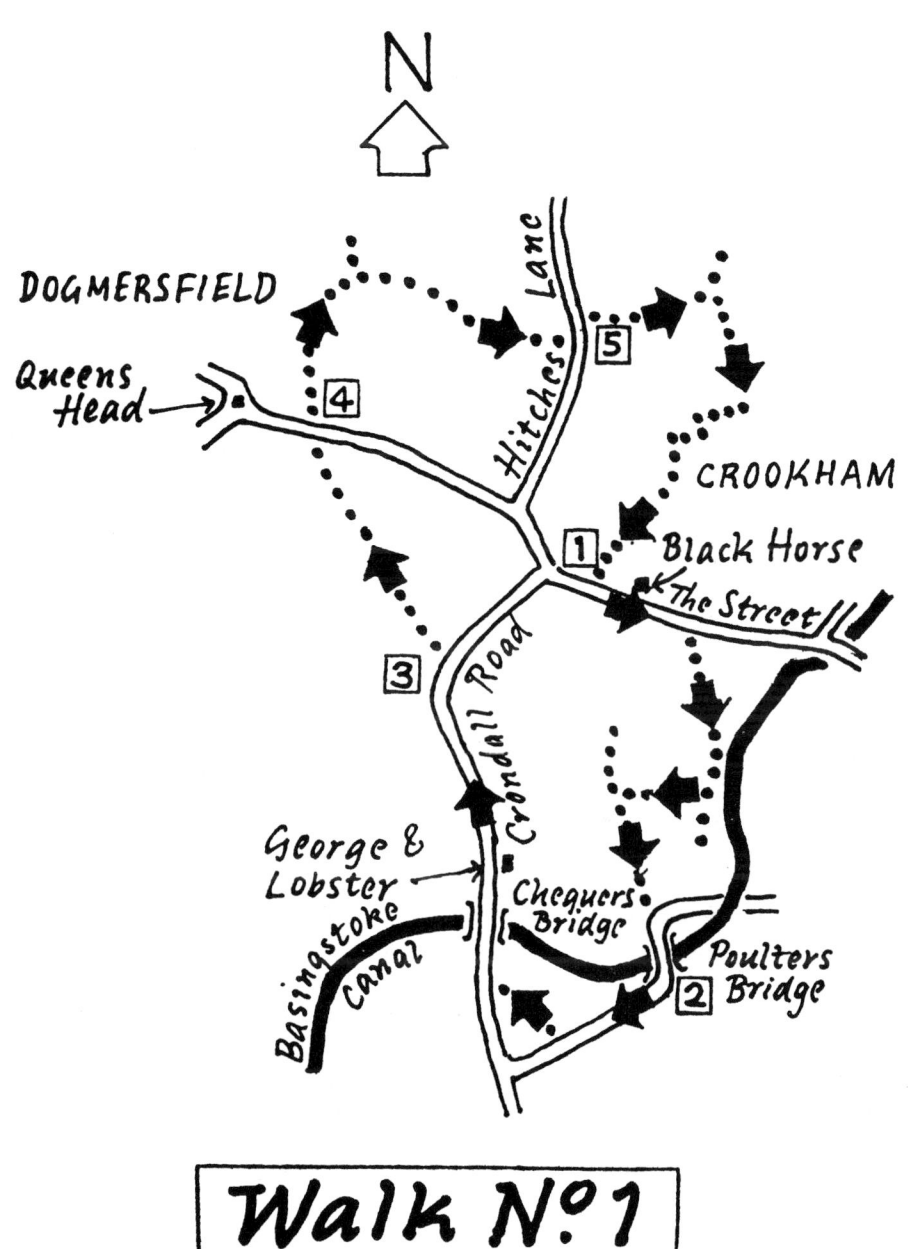

Walk No 2 BEACON HILL & EWSHOT

[4 miles, 2 hours]

1. Start from Crookham War Memorial Hall opposite The Wyvern. Go along the RH footway of Sandy Lane, after 400 yards opposite Tweseldown Road, turn R at a footpath signpost. Follow the path through the wood bearing L at a waymark post and along the path with the field on your L. At the culvert, turn L along the enclosed path that shortly opens up to a track and reaches a road.

2. Turn R along the road and just beyond the houses, turn L at a 3-fingered footpath signpost on the path with a line of oaks and a tarmac path on your L. After 200 yards, look out for a gap in the hedge on your R and turn R through it into the field. Turn L along the LHS of the field and go through a gap in the field corner to another field. In 200 yards turn L over a stile and on the path through the wood to reach Tadpole Lane.

3. Turn L along the road and in a few yards, turn R over a stile opposite a footpath signpost. Go along the RHS of the field, over a stile and keep to the field edge. [Can be wet] Cross another stile, and at the field corner cross two adjacent stiles and go along the drive passing houses to reach Beacon Hill Road.

4. Turn R up the hill for 10 yards and with extreme caution cross the busy road to a gap in the trees. Go through the conifers for 100 yards and then turn R up a steep wide track up Beacon Hill. At the top of the hill, fork R on a grass track. In due course continue by a made-up track that reaches a wide crossing track [with a metal barrier to the road on your R]. NOTE For Caesar's Camp turn L along the crossing track for about a mile.

5. Turn R at the barrier and carefully cross Beacon Hill Road to the bridleway signpost opposite on your L. Follow the track through the wood and descend along the road passing houses and The Windmill. Continue down the hill; at the T-junction, turn R at Tadpole Lane by Ewshot Village Hall. In 30 yards, turn L at a footpath signpost and go through the car park. [NOTE   The walk can be started from here]

6. Go to the L of the tennis court and over the stile; keep along the LHS of the field, through some trees and turn half R across the next field and descend on a grass path to a gap in the trees. Cross the ditch by a footbridge and turn half L on a path passing an oak tree in mid-field. Shortly fork R on the path and continue to the LH corner of the field.

7. Turn R along the road. [You have now reached the same route as the outward journey]. Opposite the 'Wakefords Park' sign, turn L along the track through the wood. Turn R at the culvert and L along Sandy Lane to return to the start or turn R along Tweseldown Road for The Tweseldown pub. [Walk can be started from the pub]

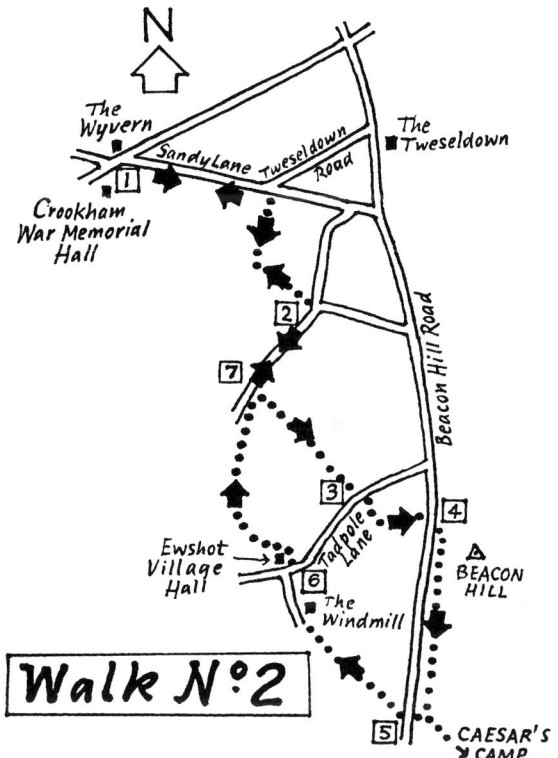

Walk Nº2

THE TWESELDOWN

Restaurant
Home Cooked a la carte menu all prepared to order and using fresh local ingredients Enjoy a two course Sunday roast dinner for £7.95, or a choice of Chef's specials.
Bar menu available lunch and evening with a choice of baguettes, sandwiches, jacket potatoes and a selection of hot dishes from the Chef's Special Board.

Parties catered for
Regular Wednesday Quiz 9pm with cash and other prizes, and rollover jackpot
For bookings and other information please call us on 01252 819110
Beacon Hill Road, Church Crookham, Hants

Walk No 3   BRAMSHOT & MINLEY

[4 miles, 2 hours]

1. Start from Bramshot railway bridge opposite the sign to Fleet Pond on the A 3014 Cove Road, Fleet. [Car parking is possible over the bridge] Turn R along the RHS of the A3014 [watch traffic] and in 100 yards cross the road carefully to the footpath signpost opposite. Follow the path through the wood with Little Coneyhurst fence on your R. At a footpath signpost, turn R along a gravel path through a tree screen to cross a track. Go ahead on the earth track across a large field to join the road at Bramshot Farm House.

2. Turn L along Bramshot Lane and in due course go through a gap by a metal gate in the road. At a wooden fence at the base of an embankment, bear R along the track. Pass under the M3 access road, turn L and follow the track to reach Minley Road via a metal barrier.

3. Turn L over the M3 bridge on the LHS of the road and turn L down a road crossing to the footway opposite. Shortly cross back over the road, pass wooden posts and go along a cycle & footway. With care cross the road by a 20 mph sign, to wooden barrier and turn L on a tarmac path that bears R and runs parallel to Minley Road. Pass the Crown & Cushion on your L [Walk can be stated from the pub] and in 250 yards reach a gate on your L.

4. Turn L through the gate, carefully cross the road to the bridleway signpost opposite. Go along the track with cottages on your R and through a gap by a wooden gate. Keep ahead on the track ignoring all side turnings. The track becomes a grass path [Look out for Minley Manor on your R through the trees - without leaves in Autumn & Winter]. Turn L at a waymark post and soon R along an enclosed path that opens up and has a tall hedge on your R. Pass under a large pylon and keep ahead on a grass track still with the hedge on your R. Leave the field by its RH corner to reach a wide gravel track.

5. Turn L along this track passing 'Out of Bounds to Troops' signs on your R. Cross a bridge over the M3, at the end of the wooden fence on your L, turn L along a track and in $\frac{1}{2}$ mile pass Bramshot Farm on your R to shortly reach the footpath used on your outward journey. Turn R on the gravel path through the wood and in a few yards at a footpath signpost, turn L on a path through the trees to pass the Little Coneyhurst fence on your L. Turn R along the A3014 [watch traffic] to return to Bramshot railway bridge.

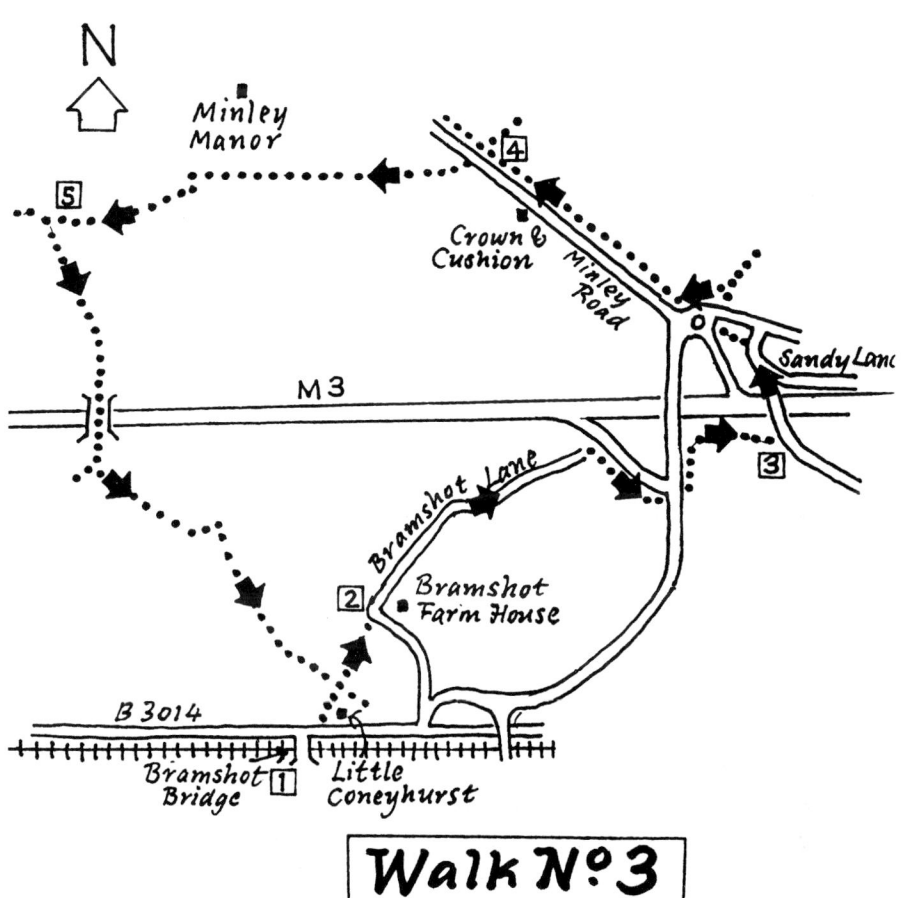

Crown & Cushion
Minley Road   Telephone: 01252 545253

Open 12 noon to 11 pm (Monday to Saturday) and 10.30 pm Sunday

Carvery Lunch served Sunday to Friday,
Bar Snacks 12 noon to 2 pm and 6 to 9.30 pm

Large Patio Area overlooking Cricket Green

Traditional Country Inn with Mead Banqueting Hall

Walk No 4   ITCHEL MILL SPRINGS

[4 miles, 2 hours]

1. Start from Crookham Wharf car park, Basingstoke Canal. Go along Crondall Road over Chequers Bridge, in 100 yards at Crondall House fork L at the footpath signpost along the track between houses that leads to a lane. Turn R along this lane and shortly turn L along Crondall Road. In 200 yards turn R along the lane to Hancocks Farm. At the FOOTPATH notice just before the farm, fork L and soon continue along the lane that leads to a track through a wood. Cross the golfers' path and continue along the lane passing Bowenhurst Golf Club on your L. Keep on the metal road and just beyond Bowenhurst Stud on your L, take the grass track on the LHS of the road. At the Plough Garage, turn R along Mill Lane. At the end of the lane go through the trees to reach the A 287.

2. Carefully cross the busy A 287 to the footpath signpost diagonally opposite and to the R of Itchel Pumping Station. Take the enclosed path, in 50 yards at an iron gate in a wire fence to your L, turn R at a waymark post along the path with the mill pond on your L [often dry]. At Itchel Mill Springs [also often dry] turn L and shortly cross a stile. Keep along the LHS of the fields; at the end of the second field, cross the stile and continue ahead on an enclosed path, then along a line of oak trees, over a stile by an iron gate and another stile to join Hyde Lane.

3. Turn L along the Hyde Lane, and at the road junction turn L along the Bowling Alley. In about 250 yards, turn R at a footpath signpost, over a stile and along the RHS of the meadow. Go over the stile in the corner and carefully cross the A 287, go 25 yards to the R to the footpath signpost close to the road junction sign. Turn L and go along the enclosed path to reach Crondall Lane.

4. Turn L along the road and 80 yards beyond Triggs, turn R at a footpath signpost, go over a stile into a field. In 30 yards turn L at a waymark post. Do not cross the River Hart but go along the LH bank of the river and cross two adjacent stiles. Go along the RHS of a large meadow, cross a stile and continue on the RHS of the next meadow. Just before the last overhead power cables, look out for and cross a footbridge on your R. Turn L and go along the river bank. In about 100 yards when the river turns L, bear half L across the meadow to a gap in the trees. Go through the metal gate and up the hill to the L of the blockhouse and head for the stile by the footpath signpost. Go over Poulters Bridge, turn L and along the towpath to return to the start.

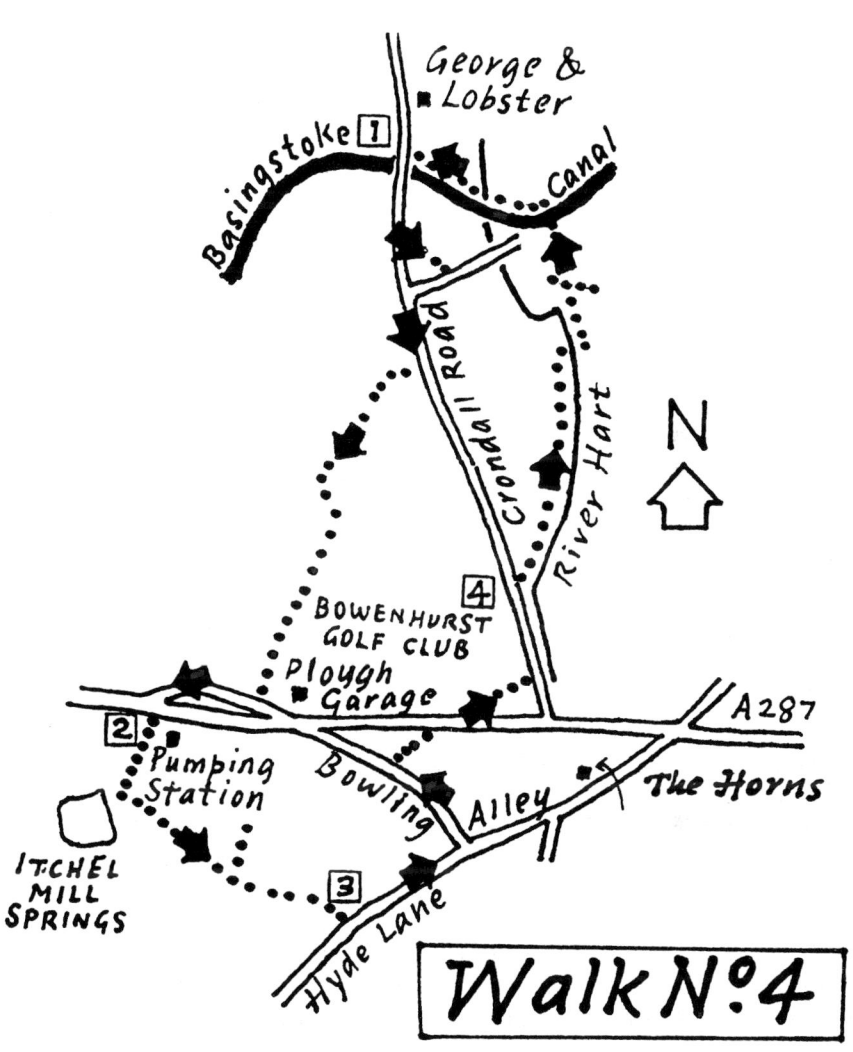

Walk No 5   CRONDALL

4 miles, 2 hours]

1. Start from Velmead Community Centre, Zebon Copse. Walk back towards the houses and turn R on the bridleway to the R of the tarmac cycleway. At the 3-fingered signpost, turn R over a stile and follow the path through trees with the stream on your L. At metal pipes, turn R and then L over a stile. Go along the LHS of the field and at the metal gate, turn L over a bridge and bear half L across the field for about 50 yards to the wire fence and then follow the River Hart on your R. In the field corner, turn R over the footbridge and then L along the LHS of a large field. Cross the stile and keep along the LHS of the next large field. Cross two stiles a short distance apart and go ahead with the River Hart on your L. Turn R at the waymark post and over the stile to Crondall Road.

2. Turn L along the road [can be busy] and with caution cross the busy A 287 to the footpath signpost opposite [definitely use the traffic island about 50 yards to your R]. Go along the tarmac track to reach and cross The Bowling Alley. Turn R along the footway, at the sharp RH bend in the road, go a few yards along Hyde Lane and turn L at a footpath signpost along an enclosed path that leads to a field. Go round the RHS of the field and pass Lefroy's Field houses to reach Pankridge Street.

3. Turn R along the road and just beyond the telephone box, turn L along Redlands Lane. [Carry straight along Pankridge Street for the Hampshire Arms] In 200 yards look out for some steps on your R; turn L over a stile opposite the steps and go along an enclosed path between fields. Cross two adjacent stiles to another field and bear half L across the field to a stile. Go along a short enclosed path crossing two footbridges. Cross another stile and go along the RHS of the field. Cross two adjacent stiles to a paddock, a further stile and two footbridges, take a short path through rough grass to a stile and another paddock. Leave the paddock by a stile in a gate and cross a further paddock and stile and then a large field to reach the A 287.

4. Cross the busy A 287 with care to a footpath signpost and footbridge opposite. Go along the LHS of Peacocks. Cross a footbridge and a stile, bear slightly R across a small field to a gap in the hedge. Continue across the larger field heading for a stile about 100 yards to the R of Old Carpenters to join Dares Lane.

5. Turn R along the road and L along Ewshot Lane by Ewshot Lodge. Continue along the lane and in 300 yards, look out for a stile on the L opposite some white posts at a RH bend in the road. Turn L over a stile and footbridge, take the footpath through an overgrown area. Shortly at a waymark post go along the RHS of the field. At the end of the field, cross a stile and go through Redfields Industrial Park.

6. Carefully cross Redfield Lane to the byway signpost opposite on the R. Go along Watery Lane past The Olde Forge Cafe. Pass a bridleway signpost and beyond Meadowview Cottage, turn R through a gap by a footpath signpost, cross a footbridge and through another gap. Keep ahead through a metal barrier on a sandy path (having crossed a tarmac path) with some houses on your R. Pass a footpath signpost and at a 3-fingered signpost, keep ahead on the enclosed track that leads to Velmead Community Centre.

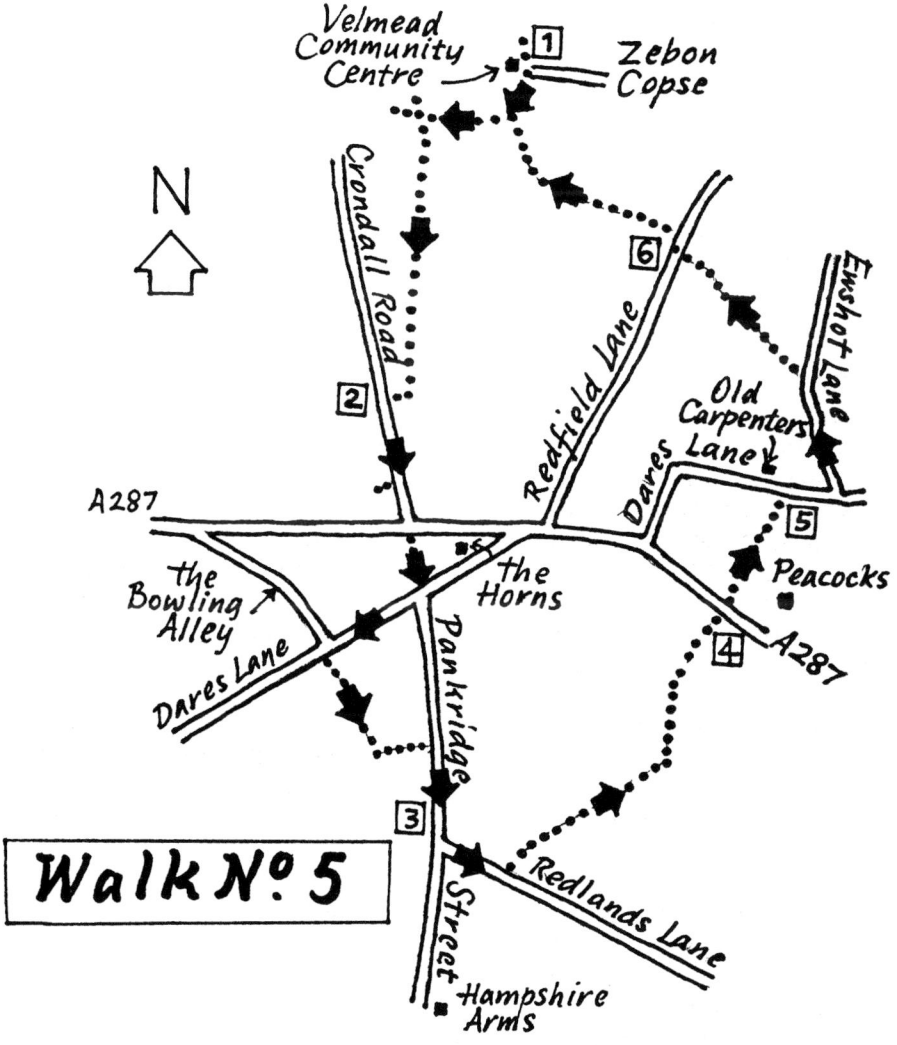

Walk No 6   BARLEY MOW & CROOKHAM

[4 miles, 2 hours]

1. Start from the Barley Mow canalside carpark, Winchfield [or the Barley Mow if you are using the pub]. Go L along the towpath away from the bridge. At Blacksmith's Bridge, leave the towpath and turn L up a track and soon bear R on an enclosed path. Go over a stile by Double Bridge Farm and cross Church Lane to the footpath signpost opposite.

2. Go over the stile and across the large field passing to the L of a large metal pylon. At the next wooden pylon [with a waymark] bear slightly L across the field aiming for a stile by a yellow post in a fence. Go along the enclosed path, cross two adjacent stiles and a further stile, go over a paddock to another stile. Turn R along the track between houses, turn L at a 2-fingered signpost, over a wooden farm bridge and through some trees. At another footpath signpost, go across a large field to a stile in its LH corner. Turn L across a small field, over a stile and sleeper footbridge, turn R along a track leading to Stroud Lane and reach Crondall Road.

3. Turn L along the road watching for traffic and in 120 yards cross a bridge with white rails. Shortly opposite Brook House, turn L over a stile by a footpath signpost to Dogmersfield. Go across the field initially with the fence on your L. Continue ahead over a stile [with a waymark] and footbridge to the next field. Head for its RH corner, cross the stile by the iron gate, turn R along a wide track between fences. At the front of the bungalow, turn R along the metalled track to reach the road.

4. Turn L along the road to Dogmersfield [keep ahead for a few yards to visit the Queens Head] and shortly turn R at a footpath signpost. Follow the enclosed path by a stream, over a stile and continue on the enclosed path. Turn L on the track over the River Hart and just beyond the farm bridge, turn R over a stile and along the track on the LHS of the field. Just before a metal gate leading to a pond, cross the stile on your L and along the RHS of the field. Soon cross an earth bridge on your R and go along the LHS of the next field. At a waymark post, enter a path through the trees. Turn L at the stile, cross a small ditch and go along the LHS of a large field. Cross two stiles and a small field, go through a wooded area to reach the road.

5. Turn R along the road and shortly at a RH bend in the road, cross carefully to a path to the RHS of the drive to Bridge House and join the canal towpath. Turn R along the towpath to return to the Barley Mow for a well earned pint!

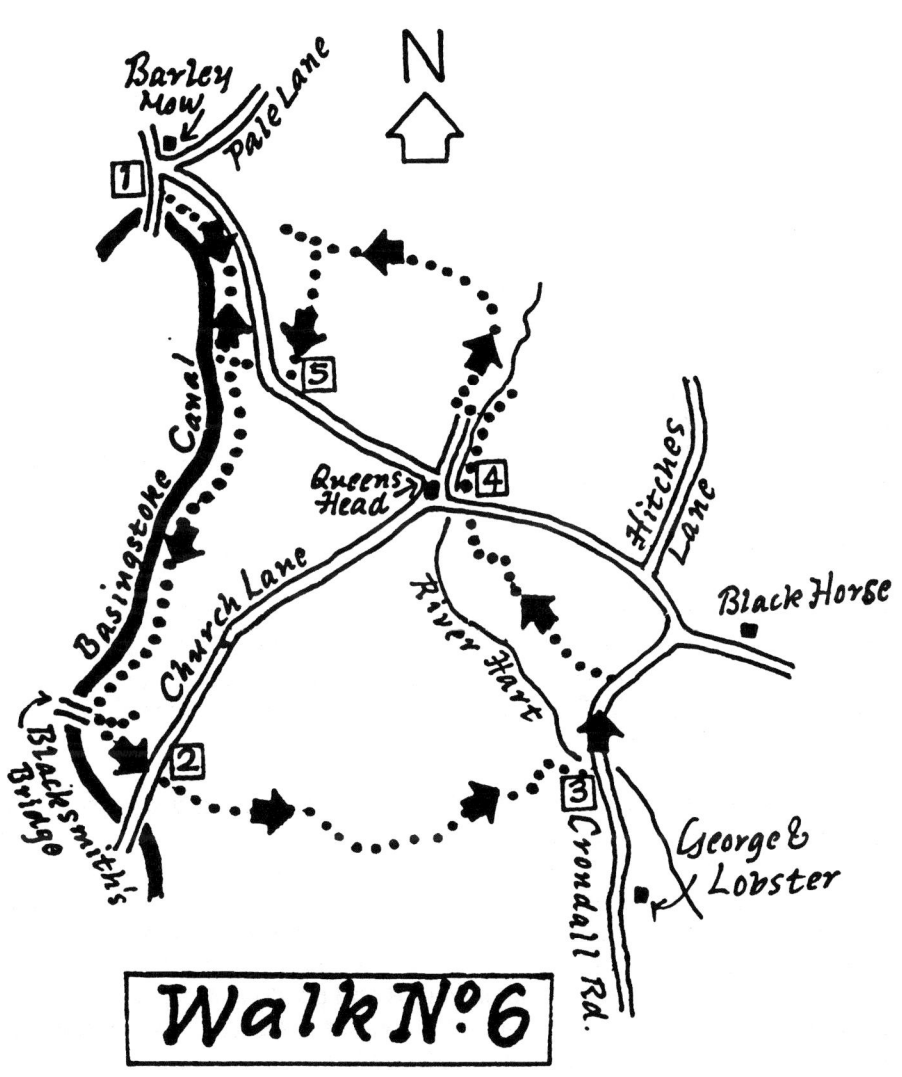

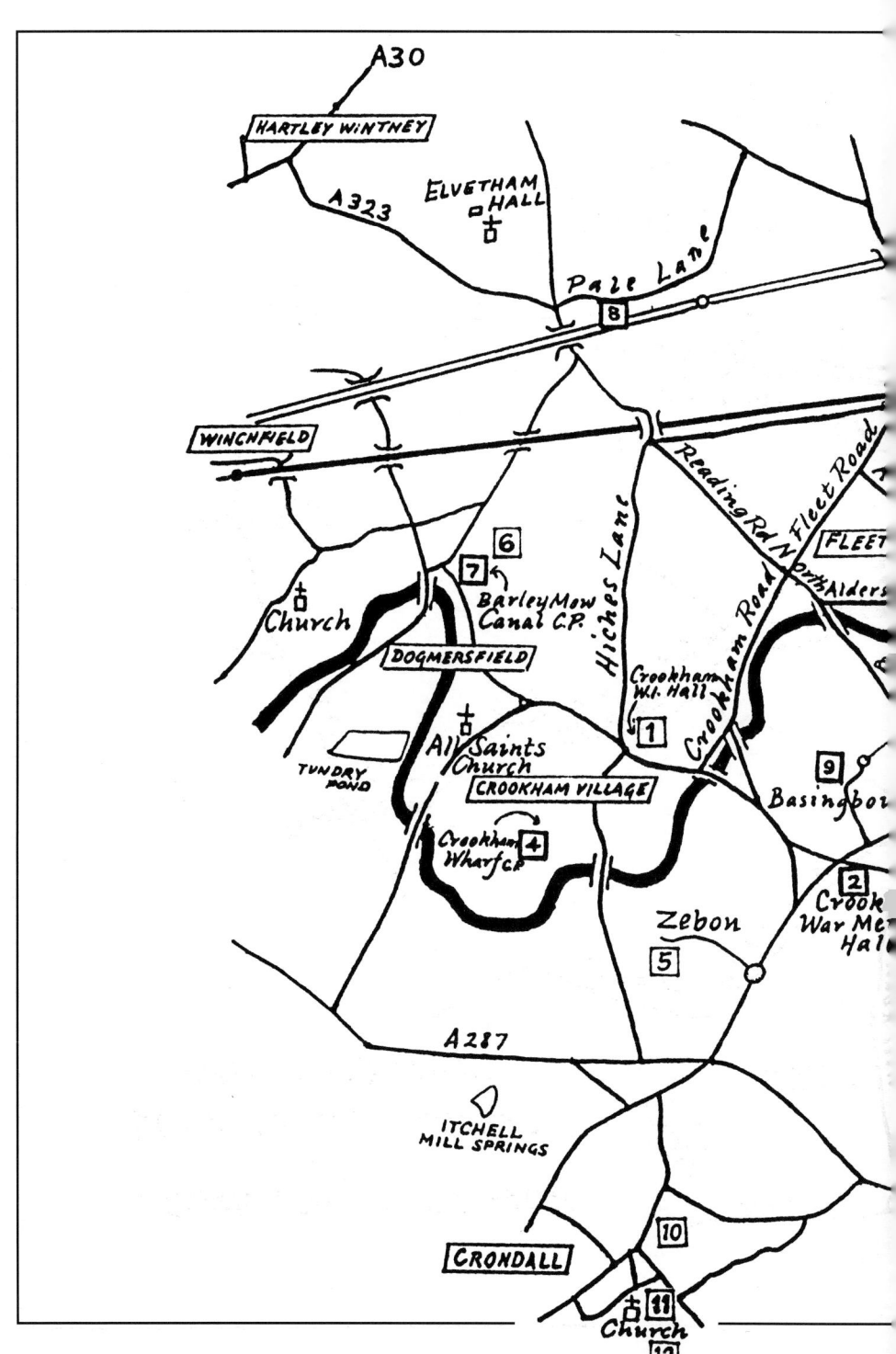

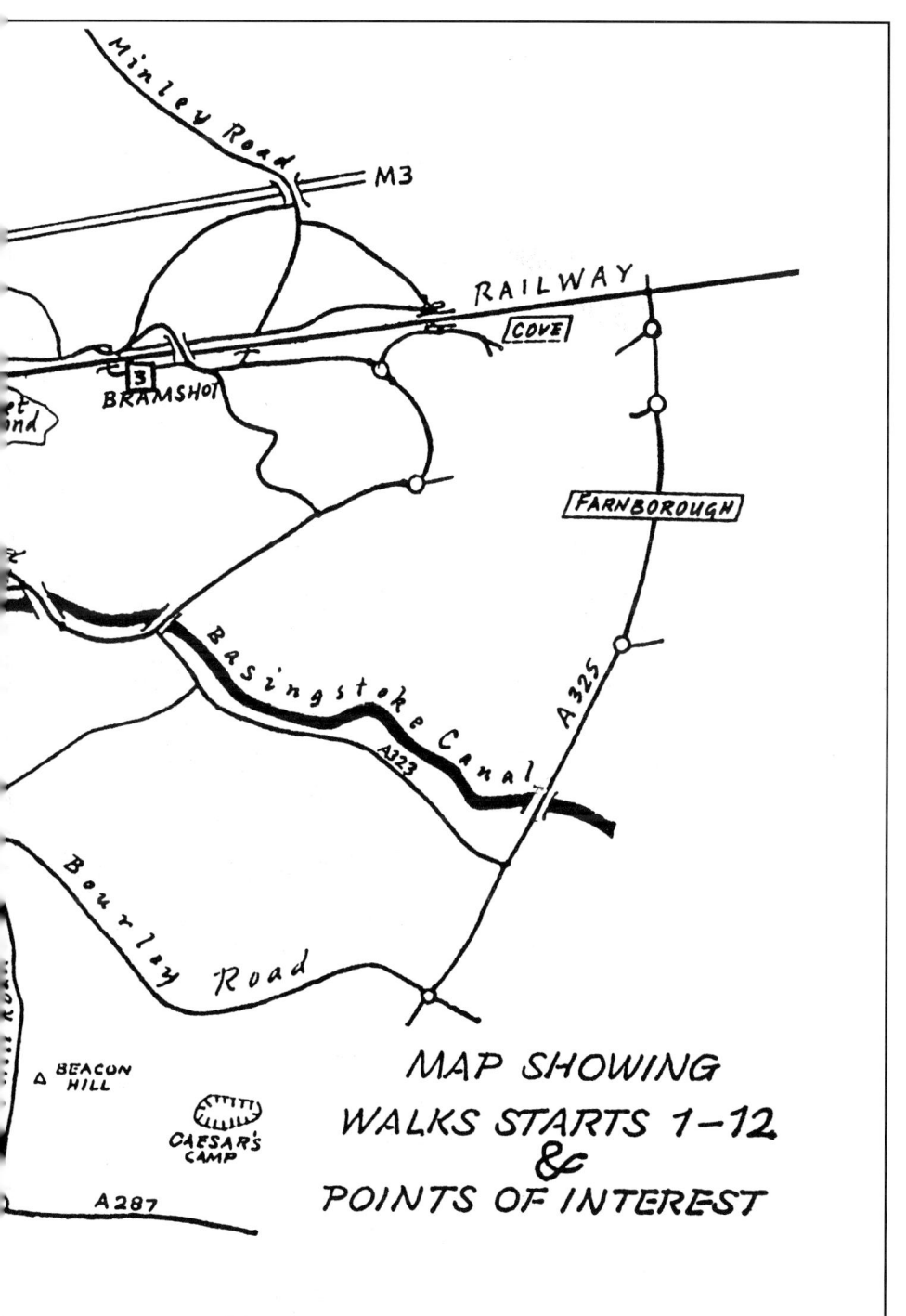

Walk No 7 WINCHFIELD & DOGMERSFIELD CHURCHES

[4 miles, 2 hours]

1. Start from the Barley Mow canalside car park, Winchfield. Turn R along the towpath under Barley Mow Bridge. At Stacey's Bridge, go R up the steps, turn R over the stile and across the field to the stile opposite. Go ahead through the wood and two adjacent squeeze posts. Shortly cross a stile and along the LHS of the field to enter the churchyard by a gate. Continue past Winchfield Church to the road.

2. Turn L along the road, ignore footpath signposts on your L and R. In $\frac{1}{2}$ mile just beyond Oak Hatch on your R, turn L at a bridleway signpost and along the track through Swans Farm. At a metal gate on your R, bear L along the track and over Sprat's Hatch Bridge to Sprat's Hatch Farm and Sprat's Hatch Lane.

3. Do not go along the lane, but turn R over the stile by a footpath signpost and then bear L across the large field [beware boggy patch] aiming for a 2-fingered signpost to the R of the wood. Turn L along the track to Tundry Pond; cross the stile by an iron gate and turn R along the edge of Tundry Pond. At the end of the pond, turn R along an enclosed path. In 100 yards, turn L over a stile to go over Blacksmith s Bridge. Shortly bear R along the enclosed track and go over a stile by Double Bridge Farm to reach Church Lane.

4. Turn L along the road [beware traffic] and in 600 yards turn L into the churchyard and pass to the R of Dogmersfield Church. Leave the churchyard and go along the enclosed path, pass the cricket ground to reach the road by the school.

5. Turn L along the road and in 100 yards at a footpath signpost, turn R along the path through trees. Go over two stiles and along the RHS of the large field. In the field corner, cross a small ditch and keep ahead through trees. Do not cross the stile on your R, but turn L along the path. In the next field corner go ahead through a line of oak trees. Beyond these oaks and just before a metal gate, go through a chicane and along the RHS of the field [head for a metal water trough], cross a stile to reach Pale Lane. Turn L along the lane and pass the Barley Mow pub, carefully cross the road to the canalside carpark.

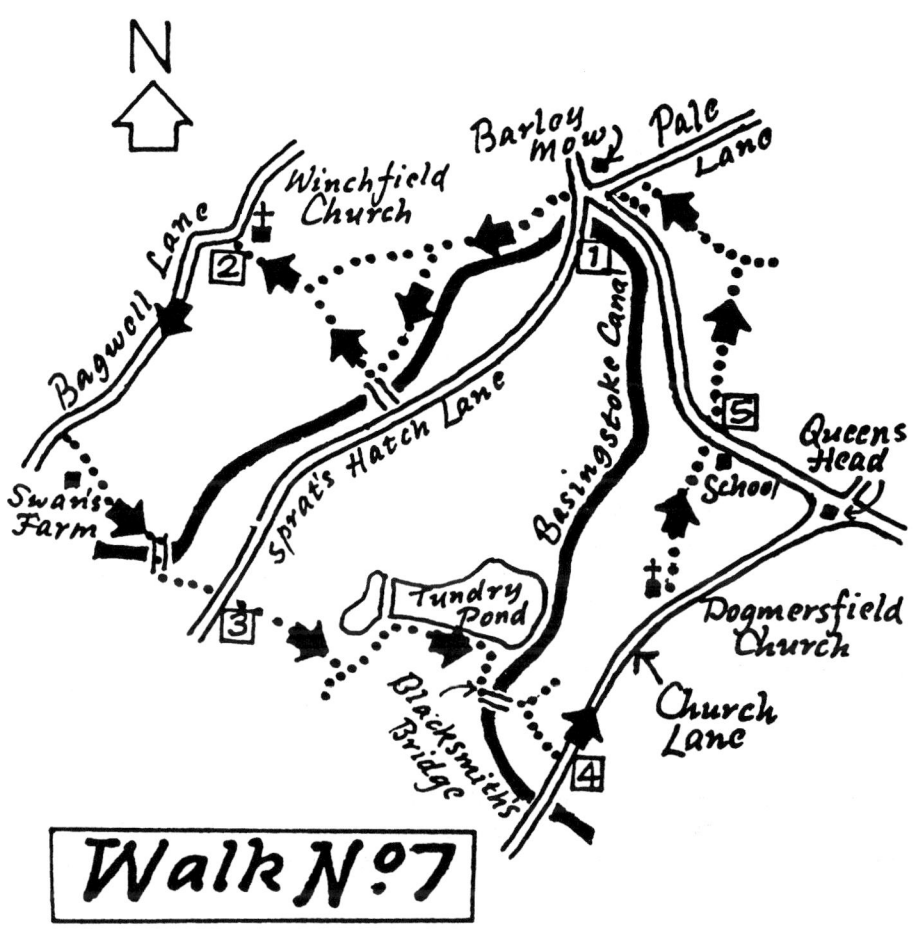

Walk No 8   ELVETHAM

[3½ miles, 1¾ hours]

1. Start from the junction of Pale Lane and Turner's Green Lane, north of the M3. Go along Turner's Green Lane passing the NO THROUGH ROAD sign. In ¼ mile turn hard L at the footpath signpost and cross the field to a gap in the hedge by a dead tree with an attached footpath sign. Go straight ahead across the next field to the L end of a hedge behind the Old Rectory. Turn R at the waymark post and follow the hedge to reach Home Farm Road through a gap in the hedge.

2. Cross the road to a footpath signpost opposite to the L and enter the field by a wooden gate. Go straight ahead across the field [aiming to the R of two wooden pylons] to a stile in a fence. Keep ahead on a path through the plantation, cross a stile and over a field to a stile on the R of a metal gate. Turn R along the track [but do not enter Elvetham Hall grounds] and L into the churchyard. Do not go beyond the church as the grounds are private. Return [but do not follow the red arrow outside the churchyard] to the road at the Old Rectory.

3. Turn L along the road [beware traffic] and go over Bakers Bridge. At a footpath signpost turn R along the track passing some cottages. Go along the RHS of two fields, pass through a gap in the hedge, turn R and follow the hedge on your R to the corner of the field. Turn R over the footbridge and follow the wood on your L. In 30 yards at the corner of the wood, turn L and go along the LHS of a large field. At Word Hill Farm barn, turn R to join a track.

4. Turn R along the track and go over the farm bridge to Turner's Green. Turn R along the road and in ¼ mile turn L at a footpath signpost on your L. Go through the squeeze posts and across the field on a path. Keep ahead on the track with the wood on your R. Enter a wood and shortly at a footpath signpost on your L, turn R through a chicane and follow the track to Pale Lane. Turn R along the road and return to the start.

NOTE Elvetham Estate provide useful footpath maps. Please keep to the paths.

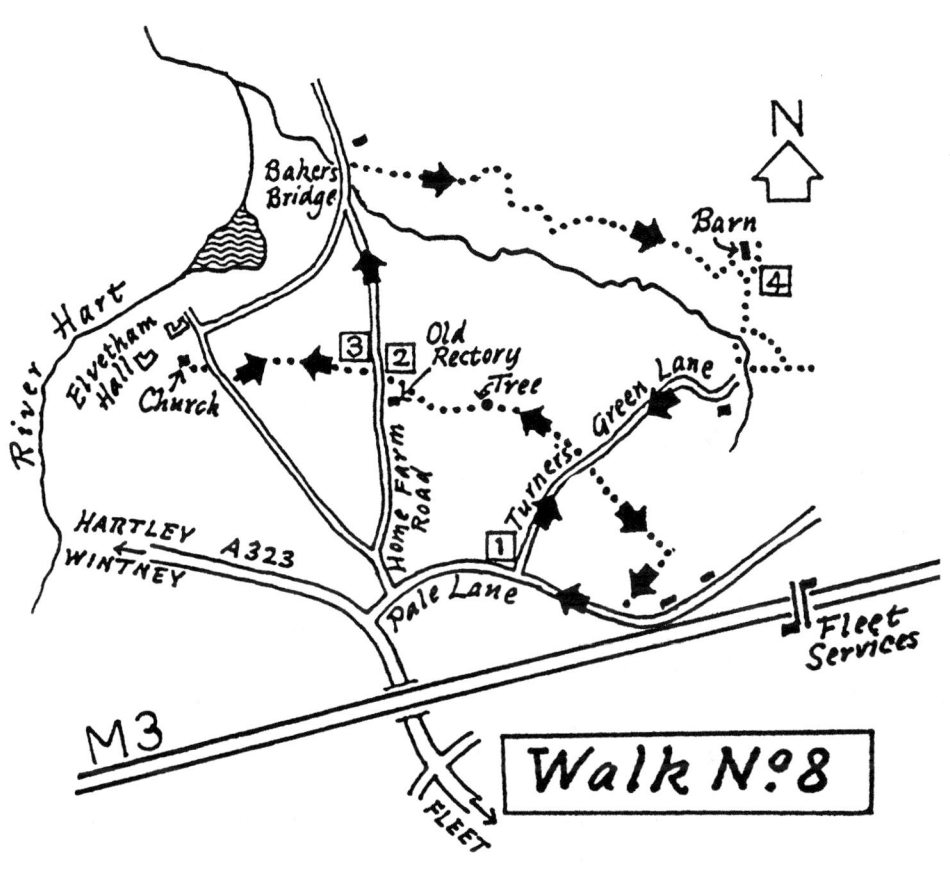

Walk No 9   BASINGBOURNE & ZEBON

[3 miles, 1½ hours]

1. Start from Basingbourne Recreation Ground. Go to the end of the road [with the football field on your R] and turn L on the path through the wood keeping straight ahead through the pine trees to reach the houses. Turn R through the bollards along the tarmac path [Award Road] to reach Gally Hill Road.

2. Turn L along the road and pass the school, cross Ferndale Road and shortly turn R across Gally Hill Road to enter the churchyard of Christ Church. Follow the paving stones to the church corner, turn R down the steps on a grass path and then L along an enclosed path to reach Gables Road. Turn L along the road and R along the footway of Redfields Lane. At the roundabout, cross Brandon Road, turn L and continue on the footpath beside Redfields Lane to reach the Olde Forge Cafe.

3. Turn R along Watery Lane. Pass a bridleway signpost and beyond Meadowview Cottage, turn R through a gap by a footpath signpost, over a footbridge and through another gap. Keep ahead through a metal barrier on a sandy path (having crossed a tarmac path) with some houses on your R . At the end of this path by a 3-fingered signpost, go ahead along the enclosed bridleway. Cross over a road to the Velmead Community Centre [walk can be started from here], pass a bridleway signpost and continue on the bridleway. In 250 yards, turn L to reach and cross the Basingstoke Canal by a swingbridge.

4. Go ahead down the track passing a 3-fingered signpost and Zephon House on your L [ignore the path on your R] and join the metalled road. Shortly as the road bears L, turn R at a footpath signpost, over a footbridge and follow the track through Peatmoor Copse. At the end of the copse, cross the stile and go along the enclosed path between fields. Cross a further stile and along the enclosed track to reach Crookham Street opposite The Black Horse.

5. Turn R along the road passing Crookham Village Stores. At Malthouse Bridge, go down the steps to the Basingstoke Canal, turn L under the bridge and along the towpath. At Coxheath Bridge, turn L up the steps to Coxheath Road. [To visit the Fox & Hounds continue along the towpath for a few minutes]

6. Carefully cross the road and turn R over the bridge and shortly L into Wickham Road. At the end of the road, bear L and go between Nos 64 & 66 on a tarmac path. Cross the footbridge and take the RH path at the fork and go through the wood. This leads to a footbridge and Basingbourne, your start.

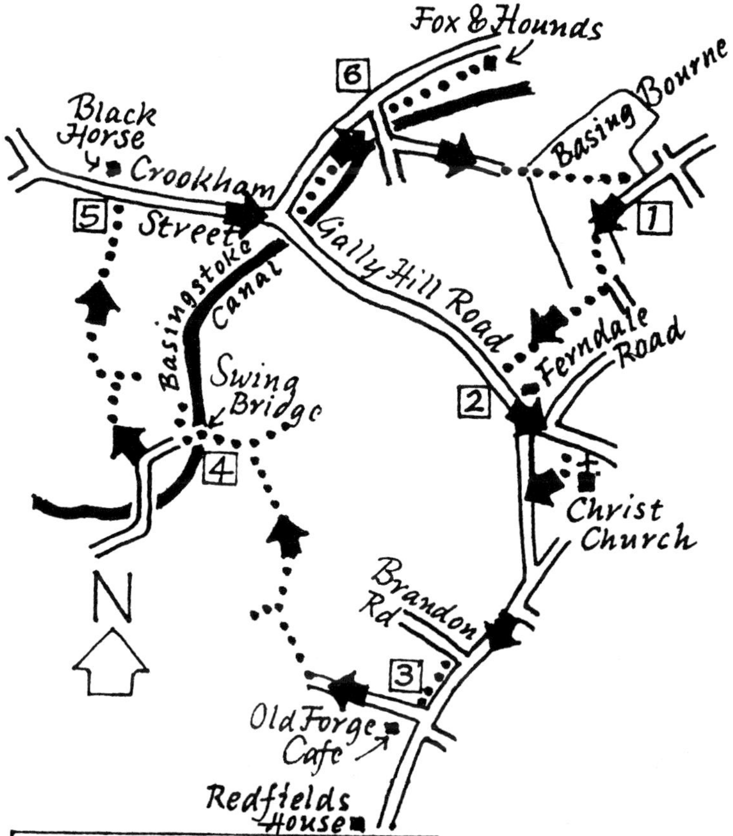

Walk No 9

Denise and Keith welcome you to the
FOX & HOUNDS

Crookham Road, Church Crookham,
Fleet, Hampshire
Fleet (01252 663686)

Recently refurbished Pub/Restaurant on the banks of the Basingstoke Canal, with a large Garden and Patio area offering quality Bar Food alongside a range of chargrilled steaks, fresh fish and speciality dishes.
Served all day from 12 noon to 9pm
Sunday Lunches a speciality

Walk No 10   CRONDALL AND THE HARROW WAY

[4 miles, 2 hours]

1. Start form The Hampshire Arms, Crondall. [Ask the landlord's permission to park] Go along the road past the redundant chapel. Turn R into Redlands Lane, at The Bourne go over a stile on the RHS by a footpath signpost and along an enclosed path. At the end of the wire fence, turn R along the RHS of the golf course. Continue along an enclosed path with the wire fence on your R. Turn R and then L following the wire fence. Do not cross the stile in the corner, but turn L along RHS of the golf course to reach Heath Lane.

2. Turn R along the road [watch traffic] At the T-junction, turn R and cross the road to the footpath signpost opposite beside Cherry Bank. Go along the enclosed path and turn L along the road. At the next T-junction turn R along the road and at the footpath signpost on the LHS, turn L along the enclosed path between Nos 26 & 27.

3. Shortly turn L at a waymark by a metal barrier and go along the LHS of a large field. Go through a gap and continue along the LHS of the next large field gradually going uphill. At the top of the hill pass but do not cross a stile on your L and continue to the corner of the field. Cross the stile in the field corner and descend by the steps to a narrow lane [the Harrow Way].

4. Turn R along the lane [beware traffic] and in 400 yards turn R at a footpath signpost by a metal gate and go along the enclosed track. Pass another metal gate on the RHS, but do not enter Barley Pound. Keep on the descending track which leads across open fields [ignore side turnings]. At the end of the large field, pass a metal gate and along Farm Lane to reach the road at Pilgrims Cottage opposite.

5. Turn R along the road passing Hook Meadow Recreation Ground. Turn L at the footpath signpost by a footpath map in the corner of the recreation ground. Go along the RHS of the recreation ground passing beside Crondall Village Hall. At the end of the wall on your R, follow the enclosed path to the road. Turn R along the road passing The Plume of Feathers and Crondall Stores, continue to return to The Hampshire Arms.

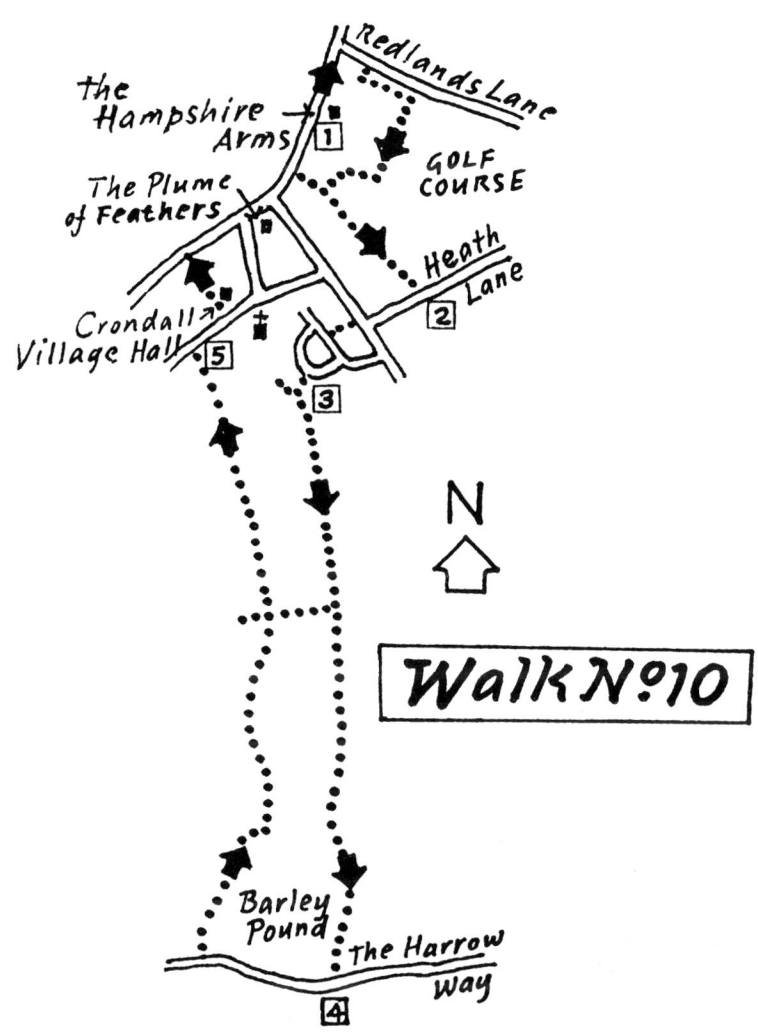

Hampshire Arms

Pankridge Street, Crondall Tel: 01252 850418

Bar food at Lunch Time 12 - 2pm
A la Carte Restaurant Evening 7pm - 9.30pm
Food Pub of the year
Large attractive Garden with petanque

Walk No 11   HORSEDOWN COMMON & THE MAULTHWAY

[4 miles, 2 hours]

1. Start from Crondall Church. Go along Croft Lane passing the church and Hook Meadow Recreation Ground on your R. Just before Farm Lane, turn R at a footpath signpost and go between a hedge and the tennis court. In a few yards turn L through a gap in the hedge and go diagonally across the field to its opposite corner to reach the road junction.

2. Go ahead on Well Road and in about 50 yards turn R at a footpath signpost, over a footbridge and along the LHS of the field [with a ditch on your L]. Turn R along the road and R again at the T-junction for a few yards to a footpath signpost.

3. Turn L along the field path [by the FOOTPATH ONLY notice] with the bank on your R. In half a mile turn R at a waymark post and then L at a second waymark post with a line of trees on your R. In about 100 yards turn R over a footbridge and then L along the LHS of the next field to reach a waymark post at the end of the field.

4. Turn L through the gap into another field and in 40 yards, turn R through a gap by a footpath signpost and along the RHS of a line of oak trees. Cross a track, through a small gate and over a stile to enter Horsedown Common. Turn L and go through the trees keeping close to the LH edge of Horsedown Common. Descend and cross a long plank bridge and go through a small gate by a stile to leave Horsedown Common. Follow the path through the copse that bears R at its end; then turn L by a stile and go along the RHS of the field to a footpath signpost in the field corner.

5. Turn L along The Maulthway that descends between steep banks and in due course becomes a metalled road. Continue along the road and fork R at a junction passing Jonathan s Kiln Cottages where a road joins from the L. Continue on this road and at the T-junction turn L down Well Road. At the next road junction, go through the gap on your R and along the LHS of the field. Continue ahead through a gap between two trees to the next field. In the field corner, turn L over a stile, down the steps and then R along the road that leads to The Plume of Feathers. Turn R along Church Street to return to the start.

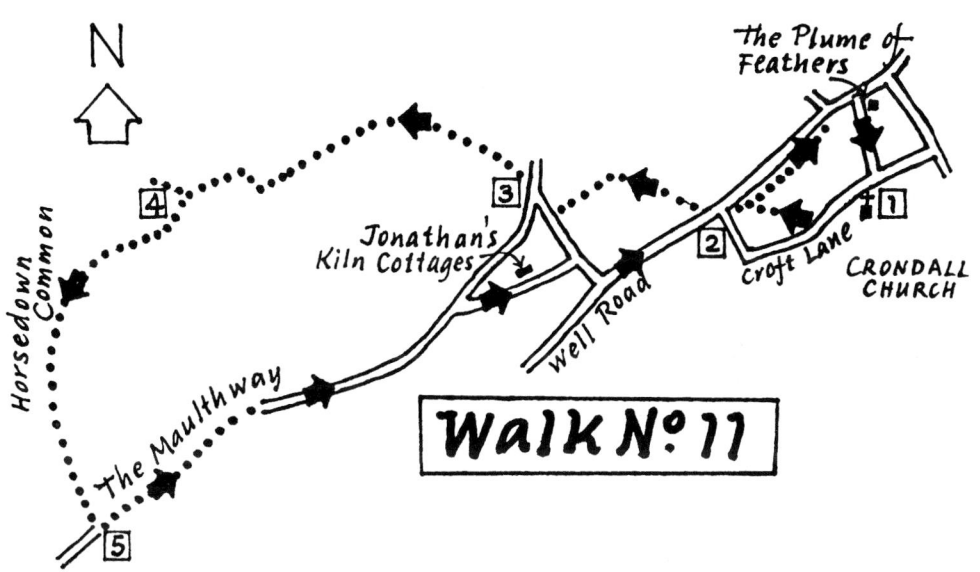

The Plume of Feathers, Crondall

Bar Food & Restaurant 11am - 3pm & 6pm - 11pm
Open all day Sunday
Traditional 16th Century Village Pub
Outside Courtyard

Walk No 12   CRONDALL & LEE WOOD

[4 miles, 2 hours]

1. Start from Crondall Church. Go along Croft Lane passing the church on your L and Hook Meadow Recreation Ground on your R. At the sharp RH bend in the road, go ahead on the track [by a footpath signpost and metal gates] and in a few yards turn L at a footpath signpost by the barns. After $\frac{1}{4}$ mile, turn R along the track [ignoring the track ahead] that leads to and then through Lee Wood. After the wood, keep along the RHS of the field on a track that re-enters another wood and passes some houses and Swanthorpe House to reach a lane.

2. Turn R along the lane and shortly at a T-junction, turn R along the road [beware traffic]. Pass Montgomery's Farm and in $\frac{1}{4}$ mile just beyond the copse on your R, turn R over a stile by a footpath signpost and go along the LHS of a large field on a path that runs parallel to the road. In the far RH field corner, turn L over a stile to the road.

3. Turn R along the road and in about 30 yards turn R at a footpath signpost and then bear L at a waymark post in the copse . Follow the path through the copse that runs parallel to the road. At the end of the copse, turn R at a 2-fingered footpath signpost and go along the RHS of a large field. In the field corner enter Lee Wood between two posts and take the path that runs close to the RH edge of the wood. On meeting a wide track, turn L along the track [used on your outward journey]

4. Just before leaving Lee Wood, turn L at a waymarked post on a path and in 25 yards bear R [do not take the path ahead] and leave the wood. Go to the R of a small tree on a path between two large fields. At the end of the large field, pass to the LHS of the barns and go ahead along Croft Lane to the church. If desired, turn L along Church Street to The Plume of Feathers for refreshments.

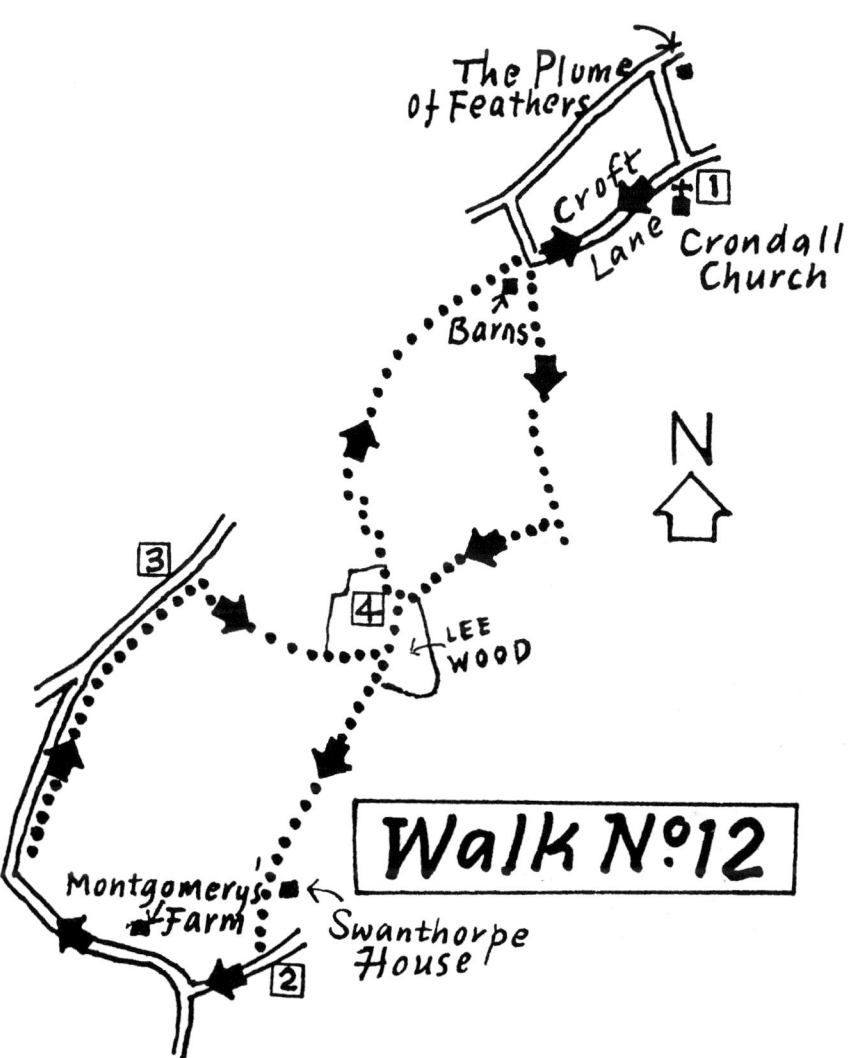

POINTS OF INTEREST

Barley Pound was a small bailey and motte castle erected by a baron in the lawless times of King Stephen early in the 12th century. Only the earth banks remain in private ownership. Roman villa pavements were found nearby, but are no longer visible. [Walk No 10]

Caesar's Camp is a pre-Roman Iron Age Hill Fort dating from about 500 BC. It lies about 590 ft above sea level and covers about 25 acres at the end of a steep-sided spur projecting from a gravel plateau. The fort is a natural strong point protected by the steep sides of the spur fortified by double banks and a deep ditch at the neck of the spur. These features have survived for 2,500 years and are clearly visible from the modern track entering the western end of the fort. The hillfort commands a magnificent view: Farnborough Airfield, Long Valley, Farnham and Aldershot; more distantly: the Hog's Back, Guildford Cathedral, Crooksbury Hill, Hindhead and to the north the Thames Valley and beyond with the Chobham Ridges to the north east. [Walk No 2]

Christ Church, Crookham Parish Church was built with funds raised by public subscription and the support of Charles Lefroy, whose family had inherited Itchel Manor, Crondall in 1818. Land was bought in Gally Hill when there were few houses nearby. The first stone was laid in March 1840 and the church was consecrated by Henry Summer, Bishop of Winchester on 31 August 1841. Anthony Cottrell Lefroy was the first curate of the new church and parish of Crookham-cum-Ewshot. Soon a group of large family houses were built around the church mainly by friends of the Lefroy and Dyson families. This gave rise to the name Church Crookham. Anthony Lefroy built the parsonage and next a school opened in 1843. The original school was set back from Gally Hill Road. Following a diphtheria epidemic in the winter of 1893-94, the school was closed and a new, enlarged school was opened in October 1894. Finally another building was erected in front of the school and dedicated by the Bishop of Guildford in 1911. The Lefroys also built the Wyvern Inn in 1854, its sign is taken from the Lefroy crest. So the Lefroys, who were Protestant French Huguenots, gave rise to the quintessential English village based on a church, pub and school! [Walk No 9]

Crondall Church All Saints dates from about 1170 and replaced an earlier Saxon church from King Alfred's time if not earlier. The font in the church is possibly Saxon and the three doorways are Norman. Originally there was a tower over the chancel arches, but the tower's weight and subsidence cracked the walls; buttresses were added in 1556 to shore up the tower. The leaning buttresses remain, but the old tower was removed in 1657. The present tower was built in 1659 costing £ 428. On the side of the entrance porch are several crosses supposedly etched by Crusaders before their long medieval journey. [Walk Nos 10 & 12]

Crown & Cushion has associations with Colonel Thomas Blood who lived at Minley Warren. In 1671 he nearly succeeded in stealing the Crown Jewels from the Tower of London. Although he escaped, he was later arrested whilst imbibing in the Crown & Cushion. This was commemorated by a topiary in front of the pub cut in the shape of a crown on a cushion, sadly no longer trimmed. Blood was granted a Royal Pardon and an estate in Ireland worth £ 500 a year. Who said crime does not pay! [Walk No 3]

Dogmersfield Church The first church - probably of Saxon origin - was close to Dogmersfield House in Dogmersfield Park and had been replaced by a Norman church which survived until 1806. Its ruins are on private land behind Floods Farm, Chalky Lane. All Saints the parish church was consecrated in 1843 following its building on a site convenient to parishioners in the newly constructed village around the old hamlet of Pilcot. Several articles were moved from the older church including a small 15th century bell, a 1590 memorial brass to Anne Powlett - an ancestor of the Mildmay family of Dogmersfield Park, and a 1562 Elizabethan chalice. [Walk No 7]

Elvetham Hall Elvetham meaning the place of the swans, was originally a Saxon defensive site on a clay hillock surrounded by impenetrable marshes. It was mentioned in the Domesday Book; Edric held it from Edward the Confessor in freehold, it was awarded to Hugh de Port by William the Conqueror. It has had many owners over the centuries and passed to John Seymour in 1426. To regain Queen Elizabeth's favour, in 1591 Edward Seymour entertained the Queen and her retinue for four days at Elvetham. An ornamental lake was created on the River Hart for the occasion and Queen Elizabeth planted an oak tree which can be seen from the public footpath to St Mary's, the former Elvetham parish church. The house passed to Baron Calthorpe in 1788, in time it fell into disrepair, was restored but burnt down in 1840. It was replaced by a hunting lodge that was developed into the present mansion in 1860. The style owes much to the influence of the European travel of 4th Baron Calthorpe. Elvetham Hall was used as an officers' hospital during the First World War. The mansion is now a conference centre. [Walk No 8]

Harrow Way is a prehistoric trade route from Kent to the West Country. It pre-dates Roman times, being in use in the Iron Age and probably much earlier. Generally the Harrow Way follows the crest lines of hills and only descends to cross rivers. The section south of Crondall is a minor road through Dippenhall and Well and gives splendid views and a sense of antiquity. [Walk No 10]

Itchel Mill was recorded in the Domesday Book in land held by the Bishop of Winchester. The mill used water from the Itchel Mill Springs and survived until about the 1850s. The mill pond and traces of mill race and Itchel Mill Springs may still be seen from the public footpath alongside. There are two artesian wells by the springs; water is siphoned from them to a deeper well at Itchel Pumping Station which since early in the 20th century has fed the local water supply. [Walk No 4]

Maulthway is another prehistoric route used eventually by drovers taking their livestock to London. Its name is derived from Maulth the Welsh word for sheep. The Maulthway branches off the Harrow Way close to the Chequers Inn at Well and goes down a sunken lane beside Horsedown Common and Swanthorpe Farm. [Walk No 11]

Minley Manor Minley, known in Saxon times as Mindeslei, had been an estate of manorial status for many centuries. The manorhouse before the present one had fallen into disrepair and the estate was bought in the mid 1850s by Raikes Currie a London Banker and MP for Northampton. The present manorhouse was built during 1858 - 60. The architect was Henry Clutton and the design was said to be inspired by the Chateau de Blois. The Curries were considered good employers and they made many improvements to the estate. The Manor was enlarged later and remained with the Currie family until death duties in the 1930s forced its sale. In 1936 the War

Department purchased the entire Minley Estate, principally as a training area. The Senior Division of the Sandhurst Staff College moved to Minley Manor following considerable interior alterations and it was re-opened in January 1939 by the Duke of Gloucester. Finally the renovated Manor was handed over to the Corps of the Royal Engineers in May 1971. Queen Elizabeth II lunched at the Manor in October 1976 when she laid the foundation stone of Gibraltar Barracks which are on the opposite side of Minley Road. [Walk No 3]

Queens Head at Dogmersfield is a 17th century coaching inn. A recent document on the wall records the arrival at the Bishop's Palace (now Dogmersfield House) of Catherine of Aragon. She met and subsequently married Prince Arthur, the eldest son of Henry VII, but he died in 1502. Soon afterwards she married his younger brother, who became Henry VIII in 1509. Catherine bore him no sons and her only surviving daughter later succeeded as Mary I. Henry VIII wished to be rid of Catherine, but the Pope refused to annul the marriage. This led to the break with Rome, the divorce of Catherine at Dunstable and the establishment of the Church of England. [Walk Nos 1, 6 & 7]

Redfields House was built in 1879. Mr Arthur Brandon a brewer from London, moved to Redfields House in 1896. He started the only successful commercial tobacco crop grown in this country which lasted for over 40 years until his death in 1937. The tobacco was grown in Barn Field, Crookham; the leaves were dried and cured in sheds on a site now occupied by light industry at Redfields Park. Stevens & Sons of Salisbury sold Blue Pryor cigarettes made from these leaves. Packets of these cigarettes contained cards showing the tobacco process in Crookham. This unique enterprise is commemorated in the names of Blue Pryor Close and Barn Field Close in the nearby Zebon Copse housing estate. During the Second World War, Redfields House was used as an Officers' Mess and subsequently a Conference Centre; it is now the new home for St Nicholas' School. [Walk No 9]

Tundry Pond is 3ft to 6ft deep and is on the site of Tundry Green Common. It was enlarged in 1808 during the landscaping of Dogmersfield Park by Sir Henry Mildmay. In the mid 18th century it was known as Wale Pond. Young fry were hatched out at the nearby Sprat's Hatch Farm and released into Tundry Pond. [Walk No 7]

Winchfield Church. St Mary's was originally built by the monks from Chertsey Abbey and has been in use since 1150. The nave, tower with 5ft thick walls and chancel are Norman; the porch was added in the 15th century, but the door is Norman. The belfry, with imitation Norman windows, was added to the tower in 1849. The font has an original Norman basin, the pulpit dates from 1634 with the nearby 400 to 500 year old pews. The chancel has a semicircular curved arch with chevron and other Norman ornamentation. On either side of the arch are 'squints' used in pre-Reformation times for the Mass to be seen. [Walk No 7]

Basingstoke Canal was completed in 1794. By the 1960s the canal was semi-derelict, but was restored as a public amenity following a campaign by the Surrey & Hampshire Canal Society. Crookham Wharf by the Chequers Bridge is now a carpark, but it was once used to transship coal and timber. Baseley's and Stacey's Bridges were named after local farming families. The Swing Bridge at Zebon Copse, Crookham is the only remaining one on the canal. [Walk Nos 1, 4, 5, 7 & 9]